Performance in Sport

Nuala Mullan and Kirk Bizley

Heinemann
LIBRARY

www.heinemann.co.uk/library
Visit our website to find out more information about Heinemann Library books.

To order:
 Phone ++44 (0) 1865 888066
 Send a fax to ++44 (0) 1865 314091
 Visit the Heinemann Bookshop at www.heinemann.co.uk/library to browse our catalogue and order online.

First published in Great Britain by Heinemann Library, Halley Court, Jordan Hill, Oxford OX2 8EJ, part of Harcourt Education. Heinemann is a registered trademark of Harcourt Education Ltd.

© Harcourt Education Ltd 1999, 2007
2nd Edition first published in paperback in 2008.
The moral right of the proprietor has been asserted.

Editorial: Andrew Farrow
Design: Joanna Hinton-Malivoire
Picture research: Hannah Taylor
Production: Duncan Gilbert

Originated by Dot Gradations Ltd
Printed and bound in China by CTPS

ISBN 978 0 431 07876 2 (hardback)
11 10 09 08 07
10 9 8 7 6 5 4 3 2 1

ISBN 978 0 431 07883 0 (paperback)
12 11 10 09 08
10 9 8 7 6 5 4 3 2 1

British Library Cataloguing in Publication Data
Mullan, Nuala and Bizley, Kirk
Performance in Sport. - 2nd ed. - (Aspects of P.E.)
612'.044
A full catalogue record for this book is available from the British Library.

Acknowledgements
The publishers would like to thank the following for permission to reproduce photographs:
Allsport pp. **8** (Chris Cole), **9** (Gray Mortimore), **10** (John Gichigi), **17** (Gray Mortimore), **26** (Mike Powell), **28** (Mike Powell), **31** (Gray Mortimore); Anthony Blake p. **39**; Corbis pp. **21** (Zefa/Kim Eriksen), **23** (Beateworks/Adrian Wilson); Dee Conway p. **34**; Empics pp. **4** (AP), **44** (PA); Harcourt Education Ltd/Gareth Boden pp. **13**, **19**, **22**, **24**, **25**, **29**, **33**, **37**; Getty Images pp. **20**, **32**, **40** (Fotopress/Michael Bradley); Allsport/Jean-Marc Loubart p. **36**; John Cleare p. **35**; Meg Sullivan p. **18**; Michael Cole Camerawork p. **45**; Mike Brett Photography p. **41**; Peter Spurrier p. **14**; Sporting Pictures (UK) Ltd pp. **11**, **30**, **43**.

Cover photograph of England cricketer Kevin Pietersen at the Ashes, 2005, reproduced with permission of Corbis (Reuters/ Mike Finn-Kelcey).

The authors and publishers would like to thank Doug Neate, Lynn Booth, Sonia Cross, Neil Fowler, Keith George, Paul Holmes, Sue Jones, Trevor Lea, Simone Lewis and Claire Palmer for their comments in the preparation of the first edition of this book; Manchester Metropolitan University for support to Nuala Mullan; Oxford Brookes University Sport and Oxford City Rugby Club for their help during photo shoots.

Kirk Bizley: To all my loyal friends and work colleagues, you know who you are!

Contents

Any words appearing in the text in bold, **like this**, are explained in the glossary.

Factors affecting performance

There are certain factors that can affect any physical performance. These factors may be:

- *sociological*
- *psychological*
- *biomechanical*
- *physiological*

Sociological factors

When you take part in any activity, especially one that is physically demanding, you can be affected by peer pressure, cultural influences, stereotyping and social environment.

Biomechanical factors

Biomechanics is the study of the forces that produce movement. Biomechanical factors have a major effect on performances that rely heavily on correct technique. The throwing events in athletics are technical events. For example, the angle at which the javelin is released affects how far it will travel. Biomechanical factors are an important part of most advanced-level P.E. courses. This book concentrates on the psychological and physiological aspects that affect performance.

Psychological factors

Psychological factors, which affect you mentally, include stress, anxiety, motivation, pressure and tension. They can have a direct effect on how well you can carry out an activity.

The crowd can affect a player's performance at any sporting event. Here, Australian triathlete Rina Hill enjoys the support of the crowd as she approaches the finishing line.

Physiological factors

Physiological factors can also have a strong influence on your performance, as they affect you physically or relate to the way in which your body works. Major physiological factors include:

- individual differences (age, gender, body type)
- fitness
- diet.

You must also take into account fatigue, illness and altitude because they will also affect your performance.

Fatigue

Fatigue occurs when your body cannot supply the energy that you need for exercise. This makes you feel tired, so you cannot perform as well as usual. There are many reasons why you may be fatigued, including lack of sleep, too much training or not eating properly. Fatigue not only affects your ability to do work but also impairs the skills that you need to use. If you are fatigued, your concentration and **coordination** are affected and you may make mistakes. This usually happens towards the end of a performance. There is also a greater risk of injury when you are fatigued. It is important to get enough rest between exercise to allow yourself to perform to the best of your ability.

Illness

If you are unwell or feeling ill, you cannot perform to the best of your ability. Many people make the mistake of continuing to train or perform when they are not well. This can lead to a longer period of illness or even a more serious illness. Again, it is important to take enough rest and allow your body to recover properly.

Altitude

Working at altitudes that are high above sea level will have a major effect on your performance. At high altitude, the pressure of air in the atmosphere is lower than at sea level. This means that it is harder for you to get air into your lungs and oxygen to your muscles. This has a negative effect on endurance events.

This is a particular problem if you are involved in mountaineering, as your endurance can be drastically reduced at very high altitude. It is also a potential problem for athletes competing at high altitudes.

If an expedition or competition is to be held at a venue that is at high altitude, many performers find it helpful to train somewhere where the conditions are similar. This can help them adjust to the differences in air pressure and means they can perform better. Athletes who live in places of high altitude or who can afford to go to these training camps have an advantage over those who cannot.

Air resistance

There is some benefit in short events and throwing events being held at high altitude, because there is less air resistance. Some of the longest-standing world records were set in these conditions. Bob Beaman's world record long jump of 8.90 metres was achieved at the Mexico Olympics in 1968 and stood until 1991, when Mike Powell jumped 8.95 metres in Tokyo.

Individual differences such as age, gender, body type and body composition are all important factors that affect performance.

Age

As you grow from a baby to an adult, many changes take place that affect your ability to perform physical activity. For example, height, body mass and strength all increase. It would be unfair, therefore, to compare young children to older children or teenagers. As adults get older, their performance is affected by changes such as a decrease in strength and **flexibility**. This is why competitions usually have several age ranges.

Gender

Men and women are physically very different and this affects their ability to do certain tasks. Before puberty boys and girls are fairly evenly matched in terms of strength. However, adult men tend to be a lot stronger than adult women. This is mainly because they have higher levels of a hormone called testosterone, which helps muscle growth. Women have smaller hearts and lungs, and more **body fat**, but are often more flexible than men. It is important to remember that these are general differences. There are some women who are stronger and fitter than many men.

Body types

Despite individual differences, it is possible to group together people who have similar body characteristics. This type of classification for people with similar body types is called **somatotyping**.

Somatotyping

Somatotyping was introduced by a U.S. scientist called W. H. Sheldon in the 1940s. Body types are categorized according to shape or form, but size is not considered. The three body types are:

- **endomorph** – a lot of fat, giving the body a rounded shape

- **mesomorph** – a lot of muscle and a broad body frame

- **ectomorph** – a thin and fragile body frame.

A person's body does not usually fit into just one of these categories, but is a mixture of all three. To assess a body type, each of the three components is scored from 1 to 7. A score of 1 means the match with that body type is very weak, a score of 7 means it is very strong. A body type classification is a three-figured code. For example, 171 means little endomorphy, extreme mesomorphy and little ectomorphy.

Women's performance

Social factors have greatly affected women's performance. For years there were many sports that were considered unsuitable for women. This limited women's sports events, which means that women have not developed to the same extent as men. In events such as long distance running and swimming, however, women's performances are getting close to men's.

Endomorph	Mesomorph	Ectomorph

 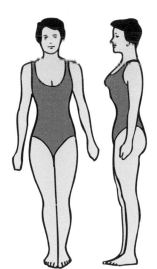 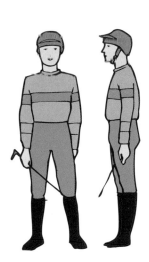

This diagram shows examples of the three body forms.

Certain body types are more suited to an activity than others. For example, ballet dancers have a very different body type to shot-putters or sumo wrestlers. As a result, the top performers in any activity often have similar body shapes. Your body type does not exclude you from doing an activity, although it is unlikely that you will become a top performer if your body type does not match the activity.

In many activities, there is a range of body types among the performers. In team sports the players' body types can affect the position in which they play. Performers of outdoor pursuits also vary greatly in body type. Climbers tend to be fairly light, but strong. Canoeists tend to have very broad shoulders.

You cannot do much to alter your body type because you inherit it from your parents. Strength training can increase your muscle mass, and changes in diet can increase or decrease your fat levels. These will have some effect on body type but major changes are not possible.

Starting young

In some countries, coaches have tried to select young children with a particular body type and have trained them to become top performers in certain sports. However, having the correct body type is not the only factor in becoming a top performer. The individual must enjoy the activity and have the will to succeed, so this approach does not always work. It is also considered unethical because the performers are selected at a young age when they have little choice in taking part.

and both are classified as overweight. One person may be carrying a lot of excess fat, whereas the other may have well-developed muscles. The first person is overweight due to being too fat, which is unhealthy, but the second person's extra weight is muscle and, therefore, perfectly healthy. A better indication of whether a person is carrying excess fat can be obtained from body composition measures, which divide the body into:

• body fat

• **lean body mass (LBM)**.

Body fat is the total amount of fat in the body and is usually expressed as a percentage. For example, if someone has 20 per cent body fat, this means 20 per cent of their weight is made up of fat.

The fat in the body is made up of essential fat and storage fat. Essential fat is needed for the body to work properly. Women need at least 10–12 per cent body fat, whereas men only need 3–5 per cent. The difference is thought to be related to women's hormones and their ability to have babies.

In sumo wrestling, most of the wrestlers are extreme endomorphs.

Body composition

You cannot change your height, except through normal growth, but you can alter your weight. There are charts you can use to compare your weight to your height to see if you are over or under weight. Every person's ideal weight will vary depending on their height, body type and **body composition**. Weight alone can be misleading. Suppose two people are the same height and weight,

Storage fat builds up beneath the skin, although there is also some fat surrounding vital organs. Surprisingly, even slim people store sufficient fat to supply enough energy for about 10 marathons!

Lean body mass (LBM) is the amount of body mass left when body fat has been subtracted from the total body mass. It is made up of bones, muscles, blood and all our organs.

Health implications

Fat plays an important role in how your body works. Carrying excess fat can cause health problems. If you have excess body fat, your heart and lungs have to work harder to supply enough energy to your body. The extra weight can also put a strain on your joints and lead to knee and hip problems. Because of this, it is important to try to keep fat levels low.

Effect on performance

For most physical activities it is an advantage to have a low percentage body fat and a high lean body mass. This means that you don't have to waste energy moving excess weight (fat) around.

The average body fat is 15–20 per cent for men and 20–25 per cent for women, although physically active people tend to have lower values. For activities such as running, dancing, hillwalking and gymnastics, where you have to carry your own weight, a low body mass with a low percentage body fat is ideal. In some sports, such as throwing events and weightlifting, a high body mass can help you develop force. However, it is still beneficial to have a low percentage body fat.

Assessment

Your body composition can be assessed by measuring the amount of fat lying under the skin. Skinfold callipers are used to measure the thickness of a fold of fat. Measurements are taken at a number of sites on the body, and a value for percentage body fat can be calculated from a table or by using a formula.

The high jump is an example of a sporting event that requires low percentage body fat and a high LBM. The heavier you are, the harder your body has to work to jump!

3 Fitness

Fitness has a major effect upon performance, and it has many different aspects. The type of fitness needed depends on the type of activity. The level of fitness you need for an activity depends on how well you want to perform. You may be fit enough to perform well at local level, but this would not be sufficient for performance at national level.

Fitness can be:

- **performance-related fitness** – being fit enough to do an activity as well as you can

- **health-related fitness** – being fit so that you can live a full and healthy life.

Some aspects of fitness are important for both performance-related fitness and health-related fitness. For example, a good level of **aerobic endurance** may be important for performance, but it is also important for health.

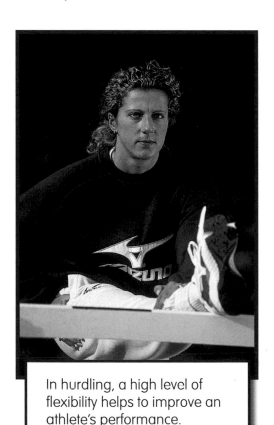

In hurdling, a high level of flexibility helps to improve an athlete's performance.

Components of fitness

- **Body composition** is the percentage of fat and **lean body mass** (anything that is not fat) that makes up your body.

- Aerobic endurance is the ability to keep exercising while using oxygen to supply energy.

- Strength can be classified as:

  - **maximum strength** – the maximum force produced in one effort

  - **muscular endurance** – the ability to perform repeated muscle contractions without tiring

  - **power** – a combination of strength and speed to give the ability to exert high levels of force over a short period of time.

- **Coordination** is the ability to put together a series of movements in an organized way, such as in a dance.

- **Balance** (the ability to keep control of the body) may be classified as:

  - **static balance** – when you hold your body in a stationary position

  - **dynamic balance** – when you maintain balance whilst moving (e.g. whilst ice skating).

- **Flexibility** is the range of movement at a joint or series of joints.

- **Speed** is the ability to move your body, or parts of it, quickly.

- **Agility** is the ability to perform a movement of your body, or part of it, rapidly. It requires elements of speed and flexibility.

Structure of a training session

If you want to improve any aspect of your fitness you will need to do some training on a regular basis. You will gain the greatest benefits from a well-structured training programme of regular training sessions. Each session needs to be carefully planned so that you get the most from it. The structure of training sessions may vary greatly, depending on the demands of the activity. However, all training sessions should have the following three basic components:

- *warm-up* – gradual preparation of your body for exercise. The first part of the warm-up should be light aerobic exercise such as jogging. This increases your heart rate, increases blood supply to your muscles and raises your body temperature. The second part of a warm-up involves

In order to become a top level swimmer, many hours of regular training is necessary.

stretching your main muscle groups and the particular muscles involved in the exercise.

- *development* – the main part of the training session, which can focus on the development of **skills**, tactics or fitness

- *cool-down* – the part of the session that aims to return your body gradually to its resting state. This part of the session also helps reduce muscle stiffness and aids recovery from exercise. The cool-down should consist of light aerobic exercise followed by stretching.

Principles of training

Performers train so that they can improve performance in their chosen activity. Training works because your body changes in response to the stresses put on it. The greater the changes, the better the improvement in performance. Training programmes have to be well designed if they are to work. If the training is too easy, no changes will occur. If it is too hard then injury or **overtraining** may occur.

There are some basic principles that should be considered when designing a training programme:

- **overload** – you must work harder than normal in order to improve. In running, for example, this can be achieved by running further or faster than usual.

- **progression** – as your fitness improves, the training needs to get harder to ensure overload is maintained and that you continue to benefit. In weight training, for example, as you get stronger you need to use more weight. The increase in training load needs to be carefully controlled so that it is not too great or too little.

- **specificity** – you plan the training specifically for the muscle group being exercised or the type of activity being performed. For example, if a rock climber wants to improve arm strength, then he or she must do training that will work the arm muscles.

- **reversibility** – if you do not maintain your training, you soon lose the benefits. Unfortunately, you tend to lose fitness a lot faster than you gain it. This means that if you have not been able to train for a period of time, you need to start training again at a level lower than you were at before you stopped.

Overload or overtraining?

The term 'overload' is often confused with overtraining, which is very different. Overtraining is when you train so hard that your body is unable to meet the demands of training. When this happens you become fatigued and your levels of training and performance deteriorate.

The training year

A well-organized coach or performer may plan their training years in advance of a major competition, expedition or dance tour. This requires a good understanding of training principles and clearly defined aims for each period. In most cases the training programme starts with a foundation period where basic fitness is built up, followed by a period of refining that fitness to a peak – ready for the event. After a major event, it is important to have a period of rest and recovery.

Individual needs

When planning a training programme it is important to consider the individual needs of the performer. This means looking at why they want to train, what they want to achieve, how much time they have available, what activities they like, and many other factors. If these are taken into consideration, the performer is more likely to benefit from the programme.

Many sports have a season when competitions are held and an off season when there are no competitions. The year is often divided into:

- pre-season training – which aims to prepare performers for the forthcoming competitive season. It involves basic foundation work, building strength and aerobic endurance.

- in-season training – which aims to ensure that performers maintain fitness throughout the season. It may also involve a period of peaking to coincide with a major competition.

- off season – which is the time of year when performers rest from their activity both physically and mentally. However, it is important that they do not lose all the fitness that they have built up during the season. To avoid this, they need to keep doing different activities.

Skills practice may form an important part of a training programme for sports such as football.

Elements of a training programme

A training programme must specify:

- **mode** – the type of activity to be done (e.g. cycling)

- **intensity** – how hard the exercise should be

- **duration** – the length of time for the training

- **frequency** – the number of training sessions per week.

FITT principle

Another way of describing the components of a training session is the FITT principle:

Frequency

Intensity

Time (duration)

Type of activity (mode).

Each of these components needs to be set so that the performer knows what to do.

Aerobic endurance

Endurance is the ability to keep exercising over a period of time.

- **Anaerobic endurance** is the ability to keep exercising without using oxygen.

- **Aerobic endurance** is the ability to keep exercising while using oxygen to supply energy. Your heart and lungs supply the oxygen so the term cardiovascular endurance is also used to describe this type of fitness.

Aerobic endurance activities, which normally involve a large muscle mass and are performed over a long period, include:

- walking

- jogging/running

- cycling

- swimming

- rowing

- aerobics

- dancing

- hillwalking.

For these types of activity you need a supply of oxygen to the working muscles. The amount of oxygen that your body takes in and uses at any time is called the volume of **oxygen uptake (VO^2)**.

Oxygen uptake

At rest you take in enough oxygen to keep you alive. When you do aerobic exercise, your heart rate and breathing rate increase. This increases the supply of oxygen to your working muscles. The harder you exercise the faster your heart rate, and the greater your oxygen uptake.

If you continue to exercise harder, you will eventually reach a point where you are not able to take in and use any more oxygen. This is called your **maximum oxygen uptake (VO^2 max)**. Soon after this is reached, exhaustion will occur as your body is not able to supply the energy you need to keep going. People with a high maximum oxygen uptake (VO^2 max) are able to perform aerobic endurance activities better than those with low VO^2 values.

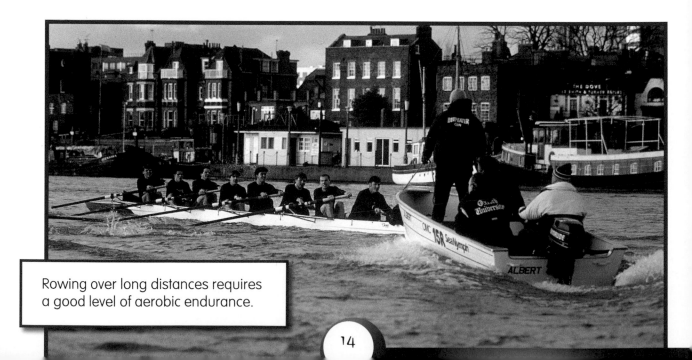

Rowing over long distances requires a good level of aerobic endurance.

Heart rate

Exercise **intensity**, heart rate and oxygen uptake are linked to each other. As exercise intensity increases, heart rate and oxygen uptake will increase until the maximum is reached. Your maximum heart rate can be estimated as:

maximum heart rate = 220 – age

Heart-rate levels are often monitored by athletes to set their training intensity.

Endurance training

The aim of endurance training is to increase the supply of oxygen to your working muscles. This means that your muscles can work harder or work for longer.

To increase this ability, endurance training needs to:

• involve a lot of muscles

• last at least 15–20 minutes, 3–5 times per week

• be hard enough for benefits to occur.

When you are training, it is difficult to know if you are working hard enough to get the full benefits. You can, however, use your heart rate to check this. To have an effect, training needs to increase the heart rate to within a certain range, called the heart-rate training zone. Endurance performers use this to make sure they are training hard enough to get most benefits. This can be done by checking the pulse, but now many athletes wear heart-rate monitors. These give a constant read-out of heart rate on a device that is worn like a watch.

Blood doping

Blood doping is banned for all performers because it is cheating. It involves removing some of your blood, storing it for a period of time and then re-injecting the same blood back into yourself. When the blood is removed your body has to produce more red blood cells to replace those that were taken. When the blood is re-injected, you end up with more red blood cells than normal. Red blood cells carry oxygen around your body so this means more oxygen can be carried, and your aerobic fitness improves.

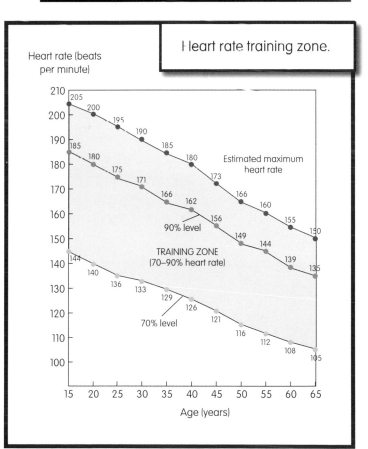

Heart rate training zone.

Effects of training

The effects of training depend on factors such as your age, fitness level before training, and the type of training. However, the main benefits of endurance training are:

- lower resting heart rate

- increased maximum oxygen uptake

- lower heart rate for a given workload

- faster recovery rate after exercise.

These changes occur because your **cardiovascular system** can work more effectively. Your heart is able to pump out more blood per beat and your muscles are able to take more oxygen from the blood than before training. This means that your heart does not have to beat as often to get enough oxygen to the muscles. As a result, your resting heart rate and your heart rate needed for a given amount of work are lower after training. Your body is able to take in more oxygen so your maximum oxygen uptake is higher. Recovery after exercise is also faster. These changes all mean that you can perform aerobic exercise better.

Types of training

There are a variety of ways in which you can do aerobic cardiovascular endurance training. Some of the main methods are continuous, interval and fartlek training.

Heart rates

A normal resting heart rate for an adult is 70 beats per minute. A highly trained individual may have a resting heart rate as low as 30 beats per minute.

Continuous training

Continuous training involves continuous exercise at a constant **speed** throughout the training session. It is also known as long, slow, distance training. For this type of training the **mode**, intensity and **duration** are:

- *mode* – can involve running, swimming, dancing, cycling or rowing depending on the purpose of the training

- *intensity* – needs to be within the heart-rate training zone (see page 15) in order to achieve full benefits

- *duration* – needs to be at least 20 minutes, but is more likely to be between 30 minutes and an hour.

This type of training helps you to exercise for longer periods of time and so is particularly good for long-distance endurance athletes such as marathon runners.

Interval training

This involves periods of work separated by rest periods in between:

- *mode* – can involve running, swimming, cycling or rowing

- *intensity* – needs to be higher than for continuous training but it depends on the event for which you are training. It needs to be hard enough to cause a heart rate at the top or above the heart-rate training zone.

- *duration* – will depend on the structure of the session. For aerobic endurance, the length of each work period is usually a few minutes.

You need to decide on the number of work periods and the length of the rest periods in between. Rest periods should be at least as long as the work periods, but they may be up to three times longer. Your heart rate can be used to set the length of the rest periods. When the heart rate has recovered to around 120 beats per minute then you should be ready for the next work period.

Interval training is very good for developing cardiovascular endurance quickly. It is also useful because the length of work and rest periods can be set to make training more like the demands of the sport. For example, it is ideal for team sports where players might work hard for a few minutes then have a rest and then have to work again.

Fartlek training

Fartlek is a Swedish word meaning 'speed play'. This type of training was devised as an alternative to continuous running:

- *mode* – usually involves running over different types of terrain (ground), for example up hills and over sand

- *intensity* – is varied by the athlete by changing speed and terrain during the session

- *duration* – is normally 30 minutes to an hour.

Fartlek training can add variety to a training programme. It also builds strength and improves

balance because of the demands of the different terrain. It is ideal training for fell runners. However, it is hard to ensure that you are working hard enough to improve your cardiovascular endurance.

Tanni Grey-Thompson was a top UK athlete for many years. She used a heart-rate monitor to ensure her training was at the correct intensity.

Testing

There are several ways that aerobic endurance (aerobic fitness) can be assessed. The higher a person's maximum oxygen uptake, the greater their aerobic endurance or fitness. Maximum oxygen uptake can be measured in a laboratory, but this requires a lot of expensive equipment and specially trained **sport scientists** to carry out the test safely and correctly.

Fortunately, there are ways in which an athlete's maximum oxygen uptake can be predicted. It is important to bear in mind, however, that these tests can only estimate values and are not as accurate as a laboratory test.

Multi-stage fitness test (bleep test)

The multi-stage fitness test is most commonly called the bleep test. In this test you have to run continuous 20-metre shuttles keeping up with a series of bleeps played aloud. At first the bleeps are fairly slow, but after each minute (approximately) a new level is reached and the speed of the bleeps increases so you have to run faster. The test ends when you can no longer keep up with the bleeps. The level and number of shuttles at which you drop out is then used to estimate your maximum oxygen uptake. People with higher levels of aerobic endurance will be able to keep going for longer.

To carry out the test you need a flat, non-slippery surface at least 20 metres long with cones to mark each end, a CD player and the multi-stage fitness test CD. The CD can be obtained from the National Coaching Foundation (see page 47).

Harvard step test

The Harvard step test is easy to set up. You have to measure your resting heart rate

The multi-stage fitness test in action.

Bleep tests

A version of the bleep test has been tried for swimmers; they have to swim lengths at a set pace. The difficulty is that it is hard for swimmers to hear anything under water. A lighting system can be used, but this is difficult to set up.

A bleep test can also be devised for cycling or wheelchair racing around an athletics track. This makes it easier and more helpful for these performers to test their aerobic fitness, rather than by running.

before the test. Then you must step on and off a bench, 30 times a minute for 5 minutes. After the test, you take your heart rate at set times during recovery. These readings are then used to determine your level of fitness. You just need a bench (about 50 cm high), a stopwatch to time the test and a way of setting the stepping rhythm. This could just be someone calling out the rate, but a metronome is more accurate. A metronome can be set to tick or bleep at a certain rhythm. It is important for people doing the test to be able to take their pulse rate accurately. Using a heart-rate monitor is very accurate but it is not essential.

Cooper 12-minute run

Many different types of running or walking tests have been devised for assessing aerobic fitness. People with greater aerobic endurance will be able to run further in a fixed time. Some of these tests are over set distances. In this case, people with greater aerobic endurance will be able to cover the distance more quickly.

To set up the test you need to mark out a track of a fixed distance, or you could use an athletics track. You have to run, jog or walk as far as possible in the 12-minute period. The distance covered is then measured. Maximum oxygen uptake can be calculated from a formula.

This can then be compared with a table showing normal values, which indicate whether a score is average, above average or below average.

The Harvard step test is a test of aerobic fitness.

Standardization

Standardization is very important for all fitness tests. When performers are being tested before and after a period of training, therefore, it is important that the test is carried out in the same place and in the same way. Any differences in their scores may otherwise be due to a difference in the surface or the way the test is set up – and not due to fitness.

Depending on the type of activity, strength and **muscular endurance** can have a major influence on performance. Most performers need strength in one way or another, so it forms a part of most training schedules.

Maximum strength

The maximum force (strength) that a muscle can develop depends on:

- *muscle size* – greater muscle size reflects a greater ability to produce force. This is why strong people have much bigger muscles.

- *muscle fibre type* – there are two main types of muscle fibres: **slow-twitch fibres** and **fast-twitch fibres**. Fast-twitch fibres are able to produce more force than slow-twitch fibres but tire more rapidly. Muscles are composed of both muscle fibre types but the proportions vary from person to person. These proportions are relatively fixed for each person, so we cannot change them. Those people with a high percentage of fast-twitch fibres (sprinters and weightlifters) will be able to produce more force than those with a high percentage of slow-twitch fibres.

- *type of muscle contraction* – there are three different types of muscle contraction and these affect how much force can be produced.

In a **concentric contraction** the muscle shortens as it develops force to move an object. In an **eccentric contraction** the muscle lengthens as force is developed. In an **isometric contraction** no movement occurs around a joint but force is still developed in the muscle. This is also referred to as static strength.

If you curl your hand up towards your shoulder, the upward movement involves a concentric contraction of the biceps muscles at the front of the upper arm. Lowering your hand back down involves an eccentric contraction of the biceps. If you stop moving and hold your hand in a static position, that involves an isometric contraction of the biceps.

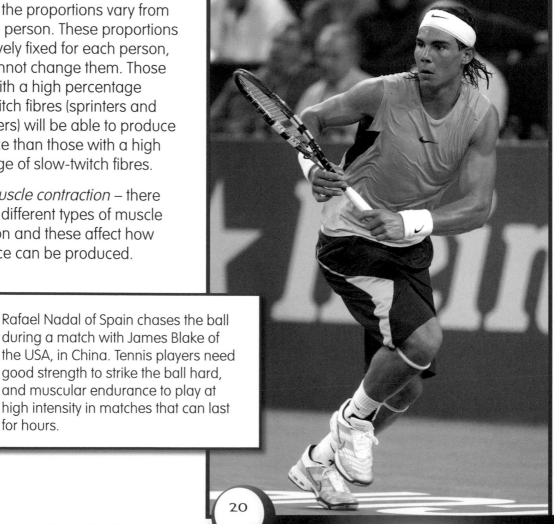

Rafael Nadal of Spain chases the ball during a match with James Blake of the USA, in China. Tennis players need good strength to strike the ball hard, and muscular endurance to play at high intensity in matches that can last for hours.

Most force can be developed by a muscle during an eccentric contraction, less by an isometric contraction, and the least force can be developed during a concentric contraction.

Muscular endurance

Muscular endurance is the ability to perform repeated muscle contractions without tiring. In a lot of activities, such as canoeing, you have to repeat similar movements over and over again. If the muscles involved do not have a high enough level of muscular endurance they will start to tire. The quality of your movement will then start to reduce. Soon you will be unable to do the movement. This is called muscle fatigue. Your muscles start to feel sore and your performance deteriorates. This type of strength is also known as dynamic strength.

You can improve your muscular endurance through training, but your ability to improve depends on your muscle fibre types. Fast-twitch fibres are able to generate more force than slow-twitch fibres, but tire more quickly.

Exercises using free weights can increase strength. It is important to work with a training partner, particularly when using heavy weights, so that the exercises can be done safely.

Slow-twitch fibres do not generate as much force but do not tire as quickly, therefore they are better suited for muscular endurance. The proportions of these fibres in your muscle will affect how well it responds to endurance training.

Strength training

Strength training may be aimed at:

- **maximum strength** – to improve the maximum amount of force that can be exerted by a muscle or muscle group

- muscular endurance – to increase the ability of the muscle to perform repeated contractions without fatigue.

The training methods are quite similar but the way in which the training sessions are structured will vary depending on the aims of your training.

Maximum strength

When training for maximum strength it is important that you are not too tired to put maximum effort into each lift. You need to take enough rest between work periods to allow yourself to work at your maximum and get full benefit from the session. Rest between sets is normally 3–5 minutes.

Effects of training

The changes that take place as a result of strength training depend on the type and level of your training:

- *increased muscle size* – as a muscle gets stronger, it will increase in size. This means that the muscle can produce more force.

- *nervous system changes* – each muscle contraction requires a **nerve impulse**. As a result of strength training, the nervous system is able to produce and control the muscle contractions more efficiently. This helps increase strength.

- ***body composition*** *changes* – as training progresses, the amount of **lean body mass** (anything except fat) increases and **body fat** may reduce. A lot of people think that fat changes to muscle. This is not true. More muscle is formed and fat is reduced but it cannot change into muscle!

There are also changes in the amount of substances stored in the muscle, which means that more energy can be produced.

Types of training

To increase the strength of a muscle you must work it against a resistance greater than it is used to (the principle of **overload** – see page 12). At first your own body weight may be enough resistance but as you get stronger additional resistance will be required. A variety of methods can be used.

Circuit training

Circuit training involves doing a series of different exercises and then repeating the whole series a number of times. Each series of exercises is called a circuit. Circuit training is not just for development of strength. Depending on the types of exercise included, it can also be used to increase **aerobic endurance** or for **skills** training.

Circuit training can be a good method for training large groups.

Each exercise is performed for a set number of times or for a set **duration**. You move round from one exercise to another, with a short rest in between, until you have done all the exercises. This is one circuit, and it can then be repeated a number of times. The types of exercise that are included in a strength or muscular endurance circuit include press-ups, sit-ups, squats, triceps dips, star jumps, bench jumps, skipping, leg raises and shuttle runs.

Weight training

This involves lifting weights to improve strength. The weights provide the added resistance to increase strength. A weight-training programme is based on the same components as any training session: **mode**, duration and **intensity**. Because weight training is not continuous exercise the session is divided into work periods and rest periods, rather like interval training. A series of different exercises is performed in any one session. The work periods for each exercise are made up of **repetitions** and **sets**:

• repetition – one repetition is lifting and lowering a weight once. A number of repetitions (reps) are performed, one after another, with no rest in between.

• set – a set is made up of a number of repetitions. Each time you complete your repetitions of an exercise you have done a set. A rest period is taken between sets.

The intensity of the training is based on the weight lifted, which also depends on the reason for training. To train for maximum strength you need to use heavy weights and do low numbers of reps and several sets. Training for muscular endurance involves using lighter weights but doing a high number of repetitions and two to three sets.

Circuit training in groups

Circuit training is a good method of training for large groups such as teams. A lot of people can train together and little equipment is required. However, all those taking part must stick to the same basic structure and sometimes this does not suit everyone.

Most leisure centres have a gym equipped with a variety of machines for strength and endurance training.

Isotonic training

In isotonic training, weights are lifted and lowered. This means that there are concentric and eccentric contractions taking place. The amount of weight remains constant throughout the movement. This is probably the most common type of training and can be done either with free weights or with fixed weights.

Dumb-bells and barbells are not attached to a machine or stand so these, and similar equipment, are called free weights. They have been shown to produce greater strength benefits than fixed weights. They require a lot of **balance** and control and, therefore, more muscles are involved. Their main disadvantage is that because they are not attached to a stand there is more chance of an accident. However, if you learn and follow correct technique, and you train with a partner, the risk of an accident is greatly reduced.

Fixed weights are attached to a stand or machine and, therefore, are safer to use.

Fixed weights isolate muscles and require less skill than free weights, which makes it easier to learn to use them. Most people who have not weight trained before use fixed weights. Whether using free or fixed weights it is essential for you to get proper instruction before starting a programme. Most gyms insist that you have your first session with an instructor.

Isometric training

Isometric training involves isometric contractions where force is exerted against an immovable resistance. No movement takes place, but force is developed in the muscle and this has a training effect. The main limitation of this type of training is that the strength gains only occur at the joint angle at which the exercise was performed. However, it is still useful for movements where force needs to be developed in a fixed position (e.g. in gymnastics).

Press-ups can be used as a test of muscular endurance, and also to measure personal progress.

Testing

Assessment of strength will obviously vary depending on which aspect of strength you are trying to develop.

Muscular endurance tests

Muscular endurance tests involve either doing as many repetitions of an exercise as you can in a fixed time, or performing repetitions of an exercise until you are no longer able to continue.

The exercises that can be used include press-ups, sit-ups, chin-ups, and dips (arm bends on parallel bars). For all of these tests it is important that you have a standard for how they should be done. For example, with press-ups you must decide how far the person has to lower or push up, and stick to it. If you don't have this standard, people can score highly by doing an easier version of the exercise.

Performance on all these tests will be affected by individual differences such as height, body mass and length of limbs. It is therefore better to use them to monitor your own progress rather than for comparing one person to another.

Muscular strength tests

Muscular strength can be measured in two main ways:

• Measure the maximum weight that a performer can lift on a certain exercise. The person being tested must be used to lifting weights, otherwise they may hurt themselves through incorrect technique. The results will only reflect the strength of the muscles involved in the exercise, not other muscles. This is why several exercises are often used.

• Use a special piece of equipment called a **dynamometer**. This measures the force exerted against an immovable resistance, and so it measures isometric strength. The most common type is called a handgrip dynamometer. To use one, you have to squeeze the handle as hard as possible; the dynamometer measures the force exerted. This is a simple test to do but, because it only involves a small group of muscles and is isometric, it is not a good indicator of total body strength.

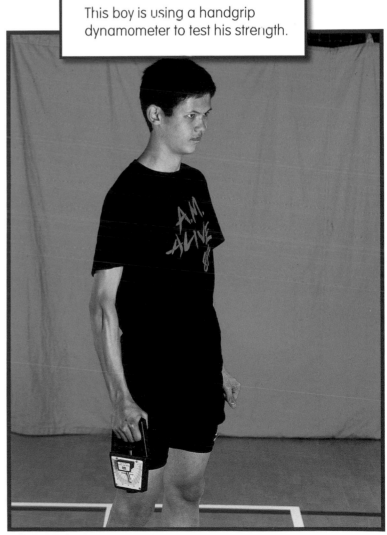

This boy is using a handgrip dynamometer to test his strength.

6) Power

Power is a combination of strength and **speed**. It is the ability to exert high levels of force over a short period of time. Power is sometimes described as explosive strength. Power is required in any movement that is performed at speed. The following activities all require a certain level of power:

• throwing

• kicking

• jumping, leaping and bounding

• sprinting

• gymnastic activities.

Power training

Power is a combination of strength and speed so, in general terms, an increase in either of these things will improve power performance. It is not quite that simple, however, because the key aspect of power is being able to combine strength with speed. If you train using heavy weights, then your speed of movement will necessarily be slower than if you use a lighter weight. The problem is that, while your body will get used to the heavier weights it will also adjust to the slower speed. Therefore, you need a balance between strength and speed.

In general, lighter weights are used so that they can be moved at speed.

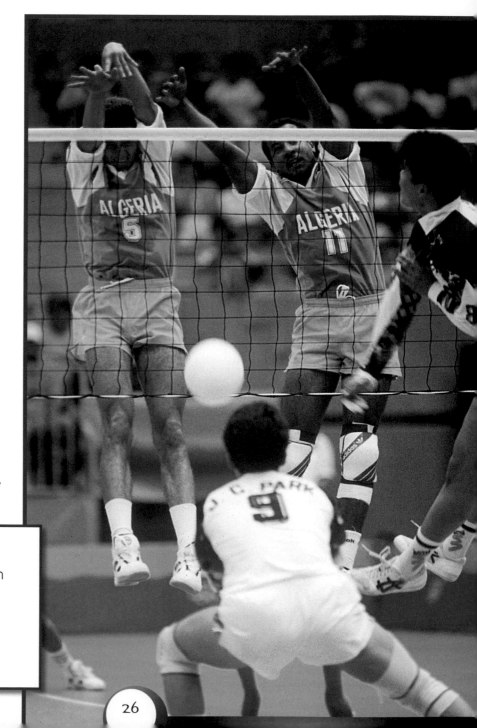

Volleyball players need a lot of power in their legs to jump high above the net. Plyometrics (see page 27) is an important part of volleyball players' training to develop the power they need.

When training for power it is important that you are not too tired to perform each movement at maximum effort. You must take enough rest between **sets** to allow yourself to work at your maximum rate and get the most benefit from the session.

Effects of training

Power training enables you to exert more strength at speed. There are two main changes that occur:

• *increased speed of contraction* – the speed of **nerve impulses** to the muscles increases, which increases the speed of contraction

• *increased force* – the amount of force that can be generated at a certain speed increases.

Types of training

There are several ways to train for power, including weight training, plyometrics and training with a medicine ball.

Weight training

Power can be developed through weight training, usually in the form of isotonic weight training. However, the structure of the session is different from that which you would use if you were weight training for **maximum strength** or **muscular endurance**. With power training, the technique is different. The weight should be lifted as fast as possible and then lowered slowly. The weights used are lighter than those used for strength development, so that speed can be developed.

Plyometrics

Plyometric training involves jumping and bounding activities that require you to exert force at speed. This type of training is used a lot by track and field athletes, but it is also useful for any sports involving jumping. In plyometrics, your muscles have to control the initial movement and then exert force in the opposite direction. For example, a common exercise is a drop jump where you stand on a bench, then drop to the floor and jump back up into the air. The first movement as you land involves an **eccentric contraction** to stop you from collapsing. The second movement, when you jump up into the air, involves a **concentric contraction**.

In all plyometric exercises the emphasis is on developing as much force as possible and spending as little time as possible in contact with the ground. The difficulty is to do this whilst maintaining control, **balance** and posture.

Due to the high forces involved in plyometrics this training should not be done until the athlete has developed sufficient strength to be able to cope. The technique is also very important, so it is essential to learn the exercises properly before doing them at maximum effort.

Improving power

Plyometrics form an important part of a volleyball player's training programme. The ability to jump high and to hit the ball fast are crucial factors affecting performance. Plyometrics are used to improve power.

Training with a medicine ball

Jumping and bounding plyometric exercises involve your leg muscles. Medicine ball work is a good way of exercising your upper body muscles. Medicine balls are much heavier than netballs or footballs and come in different weights. Catching and throwing exercises work your upper body in the same way as jumping works your lower body.

When catching, you have to control the ball as it approaches and then throw it again as quickly as possible. Again the aim is maximum force and minimum contact time whilst maintaining balance, control and technique. This is useful training for netball and basketball players.

Testing power

To measure power accurately, the force and speed (velocity) must be measured.

power = force x velocity

This is difficult to do, and some of the tests that are used are not true measures of power. Instead they are based on the assumption that a more powerful person will perform better on the test. Two tests that are commonly used are the vertical jump test and the standing broad jump test.

Vertical jump test

The vertical jump test is also known as the sergeant jump. It tests your ability to jump vertically, which shows your leg power.

The test is very simple to do, but hard to do accurately. You stand with one side close to a wall and reach up with the hand on that side of you. You touch the wall as high up as possible while keeping both feet on the floor.

Discus throwers need a lot of power to throw the discus as far as possible.

This point is marked. It is easier for you to mark the height if you have chalk on your hand. You can then relax that arm. When ready, you jump up and touch the wall as high up as you can. The distance between the two marks is recorded and used to show power. The more powerful your legs are the higher your jump will be. The actual way to perform the jump varies according to different methods. The important thing is to standardize the method you select each time you do the test.

One problem with the test is that you may not hit the wall when you are at your highest point, but on the way up or down. To help eliminate this problem there are now jump mats available that can be used to measure vertical jump more accurately. These mats are like pressure pads. You stand on the mat and perform a vertical jump. The mat detects the period when you are in the air and times it. The time is used to calculate the height jumped.

Standing broad jump test

The standing broad jump test measures how far you can jump in the horizontal direction. It is used as an indirect measurement of leg power. Start with both feet behind a line, shoulder-width apart and then jump as far forward as possible. The distance is measured from the line to where the back heel lands. It is a good idea to use a mat for this test, for a soft landing. You must take care that the mats are not on a slippery surface, or they could slip when you take off or land. The main problem with this test is that it depends a lot on technique. This means that you could get a higher score, because of good technique, than someone with greater leg power who has poor technique.

The vertical jump test (sergeant jump) can be used to measure leg power.

Your **speed** affects any performance that requires fast movements or reactions. Speed is the ability to move your body, or parts of it, quickly. The type of speed required may also vary considerably. Some types of speed are:

• maximum speed – which is the maximum speed that can be achieved. A sprinter may take 30–40 metres to reach maximum speed.

• acceleration speed – which is the ability to increase speed of movement rapidly even though maximum speed may not be reached. In many sports the athlete has to accelerate over short distances to reach a ball or opponent. Although they may not reach maximum speed, increased acceleration will allow them to get to where they want to go faster.

• **speed endurance** – which is the ability to perform repeated efforts without fatigue. Speed endurance relates to speed in the same way **muscular endurance** relates to strength.

Some activities, such as sprinting, rely heavily on speed whilst for others, such as long distance events, it is less important. In activities where speed is vital, athletes need to train to develop their speed and improve performance. In many activities, the speed of your limb movement is almost as important as your body speed. For example, when throwing a ball, the speed of your arm is very important.

Although you can train to improve speed, some people have a better natural ability to move at speed than others. This is due to differences in muscle fibres that are determined before birth. **Fast-twitch fibres** can contract rapidly and produce a lot of force. They are more suited to movements that require a lot of speed. People with higher percentages of fast-twitch fibres are able to move faster than those with lower percentages. To be a top-class sprinter you need to have been born with the right muscle types and to train very hard.

Javelin throwers need a high-speed arm movement to gain the most distance.

Speed training

The general aim of speed training is to enable you to move all or part of your body faster. The type of training will vary depending on which type of speed you want to improve.

Coordination plays an important role in speed movements. Unless you can control your movement, the speed you develop could be wasted. Learning a good technique is an essential part of any speed training.

As your technique improves, your speed can be increased towards maximum.

For most speed training you need to work at a speed greater than 75 per cent of your maximum. The rest periods between **repetitions** need to be long enough to allow you to repeat the movement at the required speed. If you are tired, your speed will be slower and the benefits of the training will, therefore, be reduced.

Sprinters have a high percentage of fast-twitch muscle fibres.

Indoor track cyclists spend many hours in speed training. They also use specially designed cycles and helmets to reduce wind resistance – a fraction of a second saved could mean the difference between winning and losing.

Effects of speed training

How can you develop a well-designed speed training programme that will result in increases in speed of movement?

During speed training, your body has to produce energy in the muscles very quickly. After training the muscles involved can produce more energy at any one time, therefore speed is increased.

Any movement requires both a muscle contraction and a **nerve impulse**. This impulse carries information from the nervous system that tells the muscle to contract. As a result of training these impulses travel faster to the muscle and the movement takes place sooner.

Types of training

Maximum speed

To increase maximum speed you need to train at speeds near your maximum.

The sprints you do must therefore give you time to reach your maximum speed. Remember that it can take a sprinter 30–40 metres to reach maximum speed, so the sprints have to be quite long, which is very tiring. To overcome this problem, you could use rolling starts. Then you will build speed up gradually and run the last section at top speed. Because the build-up of speed is gradual it is less tiring.

Another method of overcoming the problem is to do down-hill sprints, so that you reach top speed sooner. They also allow you to experience speeds greater than you are used to, but you need to be able to maintain control at that speed.

In events such as shot-put, where a heavy object needs to be moved as fast as possible, the speed of movement is affected by the weight of the object. By using a lighter object in training more speed can be developed and the muscles and nerves adjust to that speed.

A sprinter's speed can be measured using timing gates.

Acceleration speed

The distance for acceleration-speed training will depend on what you are training for. In many sports the performer has to accelerate over a short distance to reach a ball, a space or an opponent. This applies particularly to court games such as tennis, squash, badminton, netball, volleyball and basketball where the court limits the area of play. In these cases it is best to practise acceleration over the sorts of distance that would be used in the game.

Assessment

Sprint tests

The simplest way to test your speed is to measure the time you take to run a set distance. If the distance is far enough for you to develop your maximum speed, this will involve acceleration and maximum speed.

Stopwatches are commonly used to time sprints, but they rely on the reactions of the operator. For more accurate timing, it is better to use wireless timing systems, which are fully automatic and are capable of recording more than 120 athletes into a memory. Wireless systems are portable, extremely accurate and reliable because they make use of infrared sensors. However, a system like this is expensive. Some schools and coaches still use an older system of **timing gates**. This system automatically measures the time when a runner breaks a beam of light at the start and finish points – at 'gates'.

Flexibility is the range of movement at a joint or a series of joints such as the spine. Flexibility is also known as suppleness or mobility. All movements require a degree of flexibility, otherwise you would not be able to move. Activities that require a great deal of flexibility include:

- dance
- gymnastics
- swimming
- martial arts
- rock climbing
- canoeing (upper body flexibility)
- ice skating
- diving.

Effects on performance

The range of movement at a joint affects the distance over which force can be developed. During a movement the work done depends on the force developed and the distance over which it acts.

work done = force x distance moved

The force depends on the strength of the individual, and the distance moved depends on the range of movement. Power is also affected by the range of movement because it is equal to the work done divided by time taken. A greater range of movement means more work can be done and more power developed.

When you are throwing a ball or other object, the greater the range of movement at your shoulder, the longer the distance over which the force acts. If more force is transferred to the ball it will travel faster. This is crucial in throwing events, such as the javelin, but also applies to most movements where power is developed.

When sprinting, your stride length is an important factor in developing speed. By increasing your flexibility, you can also improve your stride length and speed. In activities such as dance, gymnastics, trampolining and diving flexibility can help the development of power. It also allows you to perform certain movements that add to the quality of the performance. In rock climbing, flexibility helps the climber reach a foot- or hand-hold.

Dancers need a high level of flexibility to perform moves such as this.

Rock climbers need good flexibility to reach hand- and foot-holds.

Effects of training

Training can help you improve the range of movement at a joint. The amount of improvement gained depends on:

* *structure of the joint* – some joints are designed to allow more movement than others. Your shoulder and hip joints allow movement in lots of directions, but your shoulder is more flexible than your hip. Other joints, such as the knee and elbow, are restricted in their range of movement as they can only move in a few directions. In fact, trying to extend any joint beyond its natural limit could cause injury.

* *surrounding structures* – the muscles, tendons and ligaments surrounding a joint affect flexibility. Tendons are connective tissues that join muscle to bone. Ligaments join bone to bone and help hold a joint together. They should only **stretch** a little or the stability of the joint will be affected. Your tendons and muscles are elastic and will stretch up to a certain point as range of movement increases.

* *large muscle bulk* – large muscles around a joint can limit the range of movement.

For example, when a person with a very large biceps muscle bends their arm, the muscle bulk will prevent them from bringing their hand all the way to the shoulder.

* ***coordination*** – when a muscle shortens to produce a movement, the opposing muscle must relax to allow that movement to occur. This is achieved through coordinated impulses from the nervous system. After training, this coordination is improved.

Stretch reflex

There are special receptors in the muscles, tendons and ligaments that send information to the nervous system about changes in their length and tension. When a muscle is stretched quickly, receptors in the muscle sense this and cause a rapid contraction of the muscle. This is called the **stretch reflex**.

The stretch reflex occurs to prevent the muscle from being damaged by stretching too quickly. However, if the stretch is held for more than six seconds, receptors in the tendons adjust to the new length and cause a rapid relaxation. This is why if you hold a stretch for more than six seconds, you will then be able to stretch a little further.

Types of training

Stretching is the technique used to improve flexibility. Stretching is a normal part of a warm-up in preparation for performance, but this is not enough to increase flexibility to improved levels. To improve flexibility, you need to follow a stretching programme. The two main types of stretching are:

In order to reach the flexibility levels of this gymnast, a lot of training is required.

- *static stretching* – which involves stretching a muscle in a static position. You reach towards the point of maximum stretch and then hold this position for at least 6–10 seconds. After this time you should be able to stretch a little further. This is because the receptors sense that no damage is being done to the muscle and they allow a little more stretch to occur. For maximum benefits the stretch should be held for at least 30 seconds.

- *ballistic stretching* – which involves repetitive bouncing when near maximum stretch. This causes fast short contractions and relaxations of the muscle. The first time you stretch, the stretch reflex will cause the muscle to contract. If you bounce into the stretch again, you will be trying to stretch the muscle at the same time as it is trying to contract. For this reason bouncing while stretching should be avoided.

Active and passive stretching

In active stretching you move into a certain stretched position unaided. Passive stretching involves something, other than a muscle contraction, moving you into the position – for example another person, gravity or momentum. This technique must be carried out with care and only by someone with appropriate experience. You should never force someone into a stretched position.

Testing

Flexibility can be tested in a number of ways. You can test the range of movement at any joint by measuring the angle through which the joint can move, using a device called a goniometer or flexiometer that measures the angle.

Sit-and-reach test

The sit-and-reach test is a popular flexibility test that can be set up quite easily. It is a test of the flexibility in your lower back and hamstrings. You need a bench or sturdy box. Sit with both feet flat against the side of the box and legs straight. Then reach forwards to the marker with both hands and push it slowly forwards as far as possible. Hold this position for a few seconds and then relax. The distance that the marker is pushed is recorded.

This is a good test for monitoring improvements in flexibility after training. As flexibility in your lower back and hamstrings improves, the distance should increase. It is not good for comparing different performers' flexibility. This is because each person's score is affected by their body dimensions. For example, a person with short legs and long arms will do better than a person with long legs and short arms – no matter how flexible they are. Never compare yourself with others or try to compete in tests of this kind because we all have different body types that affect our flexibility.

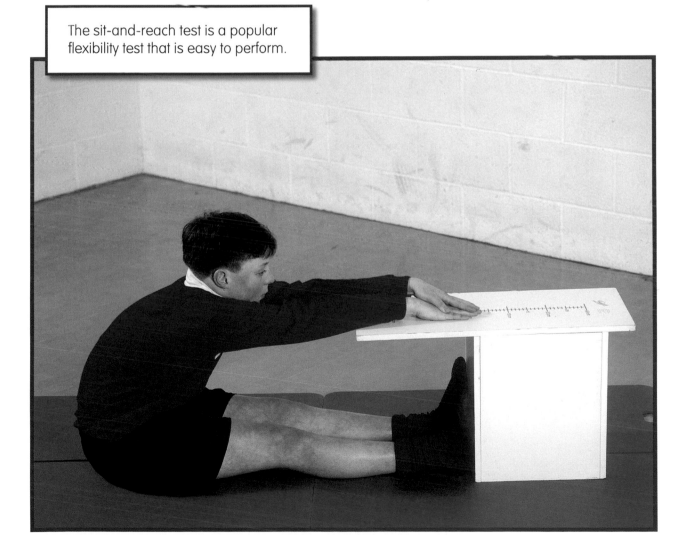

The sit-and-reach test is a popular flexibility test that is easy to perform.

9 Diet

It is important for all people, not only performers, to follow a diet that contains the right balance of foods. A healthy diet includes a variety of different foods that allow your body to function at its best. If you do not follow a good diet then you are unlikely to perform at your best. Three important concepts for healthy eating are:

- *variety* – different foods provide different nutrients. Eating a wide variety of food will help ensure you have a healthy diet.

- *balance* – eating the right proportions of different foods is vital for a balanced diet

- *moderation* – eating too much or too little of any one type of food or nutrient can be harmful.

In order to survive, you must consume food to supply your body with the nutrients it needs. The six essential nutrients are:

- carbohydrates
- fats
- proteins
- minerals
- vitamins
- water.

Different foods contain various amounts of these nutrients.

Carbohydrates

Carbohydrates are important for maintaining your body's energy stores. These are digested and used for energy. Dietary **fibre** is also a

Complex carbohydrates, such as bread, are an important part of any diet.

form of carbohydrate but it is indigestible. The two main types of carbohydrate are:

- **simple carbohydrates (sugars)** which are made up of a few sugar units. Jam, marmalade, honey, sugar, sweets and biscuits are all rich sources of simple carbohydrates. They are considered less nutritious than complex carbohydrates because they contain only small amounts of other nutrients and fibre.

- **complex carbohydrates (starches)** which are made up of many sugar units. Foods such as bread, rice, pasta and vegetables are valuable sources of complex carbohydrates. They are considered more nutritious because they also contain vitamins, minerals and fibre.

Fibre is not absorbed by your body, but it is essential because it ensures that your digestive system functions correctly. It is the non-digestible carbohydrate that forms the skeleton of plant cells. Good fibre sources include wholemeal bread, wholewheat pasta, cereals and pulses.

Fats

Fats are important sources of energy. They are stored in your body and provide insulation and protection as well as energy.

The basic component of fat is triglyceride, which consists of a glycerol base with three fatty acids attached. The three main types of fatty acid are:

- **saturated fatty acid** – mainly found in animal products such as meat, poultry and dairy products

- **monounsaturated fat** – found in peanuts and olive oil

- **polyunsaturated fat** – found in sunflower oil, soya bean oil and corn oil as well as in oily fish such as sardines, herring and mackerel.

Fat is an important nutrient but it is generally believed that we eat too much fat in our diet. This can lead to obesity and related health problems such as coronary heart disease and cancer.

Proteins

Proteins are needed by the body for growth and repair of tissues such as muscle, hair and skin. They are also used to make enzymes and hormones. Proteins are made up of simple units called **amino acids**. Protein is not normally used to provide energy for exercise but in extreme conditions, such as starvation, it may be used. In very long periods of low **intensity** exercise, protein may be used when carbohydrate supplies are very low.

There are 20 amino acids, around half of which can be made by your body (**non-essential amino acids**). There are at least nine **essential amino acids** that cannot be made by your body and so must be obtained from your diet. Animal sources of protein, such as meat, fish and dairy products, contain all the essential amino acids but tend to be high in fat. Vegetable sources, such as beans, cereals and pulses, are high in carbohydrate and fibre but contain lower amounts of some amino acids, and so a mixture of these foods is required.

Vegetarian diet

The benefits of a vegetarian diet are that it tends to be high in fibre, rich in vitamins and minerals, and low in fat. However, those on a vegetarian diet need to be careful about mixing their protein sources to ensure adequate intake of the essential amino acids. Fortunately, by combining certain foods such as cereal with milk or beans on toast, you can obtain all the amino acids.

Vitamins

Vitamins are chemical compounds needed in very small amounts to perform specific functions, but your body cannot make them.

- **Fat-soluble vitamins** – A, D, E and K – are stored in large quantities in the body.

- **Water-soluble vitamins** – B and C – are mostly involved in energy production.

Your body needs vitamins for:

- growth and maintenance of cells, skin, bones and teeth

- the breakdown of food and energy production

- the stability of the nervous system and to fight disease.

Minerals

Your body needs minerals for all the chemical processes that go on inside it that result in growth, energy production and development. Minerals are needed by the body in small amounts, but it is important that enough minerals are included in your diet. Iron,

Vitamin supplements

If you eat a variety of foods in your diet you will get an adequate supply of vitamins. Despite this, many people choose to buy expensive vitamin supplements in the belief that it will improve their health.

sodium, potassium, calcium, magnesium and phosphorus are all minerals. They affect various functions including:

- structure of bones and teeth

- muscle contraction and nerve impulse conduction

- enzyme formation (These are compounds that speed up chemical reactions.)

- fluid balance in the body

- energy processes.

Water

Water is essential for all body functions. It is the main transport mechanism of the human body conveying nutrients, waste products and hormones to the tissues. Water is also a major component of many cells. It is vital for regulation of your body temperature, absorbing heat and transferring it to your skin so it can be released to the environment. Sweating is part of this process.

Top athletes in all sports, such as these shooters from the New Zealand Silver Ferns netball team, make sure they drink fluids before, during and after a match.

Energy for exercise

During very hard exercise (high intensity) carbohydrate alone is used to supply energy. During longer, light exercise (low intensity), fat is mainly used as an energy source. There is plenty of fat stored in your body but you can only store a limited amount of carbohydrate in your muscles. It is important if you are involved in sport or exercise that you eat enough carbohydrate every day to keep your stores high. If you do not eat enough carbohydrate, these stores will not be able to produce enough energy and your performance will decline.

How much carbohydrate?

In an experiment, a way was found of enabling performers to store greater quantities of carbohydrate than before. This involved draining the body's stores of carbohydrate by training hard and eating very little carbohydrate for a few days. Then, by eating a lot of carbohydrate and doing less training, their carbohydrate stores were increased. This meant they were able to provide more energy from carbohydrate. Many athletes tried doing this a week before a long-distance event, such as the marathon, but there were a lot of problems with it. Many athletes felt tired and irritable during the low carbohydrate diet and hard training phase. Often they had not recovered fully before the event so were not feeling at their best on the day. This type of carbohydrate 'loading' is no longer recommended. Instead athletes should maintain a high carbohydrate diet throughout their training. A few days before the event the athlete should gradually reduce training so that their carbohydrate stores are high at the start of the event. This is called **tapering**.

A lot of fluid can be lost during exercise due to sweating.

Fluids and exercise

During exercise, your body produces a lot of heat. To prevent your body temperature from getting too high, you have to get rid of this heat. During exercise sweating helps to do this.

Sweating is a very effective way of losing heat but it may cause **dehydration**, which takes place when your body does not have enough water to work properly. It is possible to lose a few kilograms of body fluid during a hard exercise session. This will have a negative effect on your performance. It is important to take in extra fluid before, during and after exercise. However, drinking large quantities of fluid can cause discomfort so it is better to drink a little, often.

Psychology is the study of the mind and behaviour. Psychological factors that affect performance influence the way you think and how you behave. At the top level of performance there may be little difference between performers in terms of their physical fitness. The dividing line between who becomes a top-class performer and who does not is often down to psychological factors.

Skill

Skill is the ability to perform a movement correctly and efficiently. A skilful tennis player will be able to perform an accurate and powerful serve efficiently and correctly most of the time. Any performance is made up of a series of skills. How well you have learned these skills will affect the quality of performance.

Learning a skill

One model to explain what happens when learning or performing a skill is the **information processing model**.

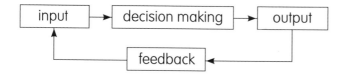

The model is used to explain how information about the performance of a skill is dealt with (processed). You receive information (input), and make a decision about what to do (decision making). Then you carry out an action (output) and receive **feedback** about the results. However, it is not quite as simple as this.

Input

When performing there are a lot of things happening around and inside you that can give you information. These are called **stimuli**. The senses are important sources of information. What you can see, smell, hear and feel are all stimuli. In ball games you can see the ball, hear it bounce and feel it as you catch it. You can also gather information about what is going on inside and around your body. **Proprioception** is the name given to your ability to sense the position of parts of your body in space.

You can only focus your attention on a limited number of stimuli at any one time, so you have to choose what to pay attention to. A skilled performer is better at selecting which stimuli to pay attention to and which to ignore. A beginner is not able to do this as well. When coaching beginners, for example, it is important not to give them too many things to think about as it may be more than they can cope with. If this happens, learning decreases.

The next stage in the information processing model is to interpret and make sense of the information received. This process is called **perception**. It may involve comparing the information with previous experiences from your memory. The more experienced a performer you are the more likely you are to recognize a certain stimulus, and to respond appropriately.

Decision making

Once you have interpreted the information received, you then have to make a decision about what action to take.

This diver needs to focus on her performance and ignore the sights and sounds around her.

This is based on the information received and your understanding of it. Once again memory is involved in this process. You can remember what happened last time you were in a similar situation, what you chose to do and what the outcome was. This will influence the decision that you make this time.

Output

The output (action taken) depends on the information received and the decision made. The movement then has to be organized and controlled. This is done through your brain, via the nerves and muscles involved in the movement.

Feedback

The result of the action you take may give you information that will affect how you perform the skill next time. This information is called feedback. In some skills using very rapid movements, there is not enough time for feedback during the action. For example, when you kick a ball, the action is finished before you receive feedback. In other skills feedback is used constantly to modify movement. When walking along a beam

in gymnastics you get continuous feedback and use this information to modify your movements. A skilled performer will be able to use this feedback more effectively than a beginner.

Feedback can also be obtained from people other than the performer. A coach or teacher will often give feedback about the performer's skill before they attempt it again. This helps the performer to learn and leads to them becoming more skilful.

Staying focused

A coach can help a beginner to focus on the right stimuli – for example, when receiving a tennis serve, to watch the stance of the opponent, the ball toss and the angle of the racket. This will also help the player to ignore irrelevant stimuli such as spectators or noise from another court.

Effect on performance

There are many factors that can affect your performance of a skill and how well you learn a skill. These can be external factors or internal factors.

External factors

Parents, coaches, friends, spectators and opponents are all examples of external factors that can affect your performance. The aim of opponents is to affect your performance negatively. They may do this tactically by restricting your movements or by putting psychological pressure on you. Opponents do this by trying to make you feel intimidated and inferior. This is described as 'psyching out' the opponent.

Although parents, coaches and friends want you to perform well, this can put pressure on you. Some people respond well to this and performance improves, but others do not.

US golfer Michelle Wie will have been under great pressure to make this putt at the Women's British Open. Success often depends on being focused and confident.

Internal factors

Your personality, confidence and motivation will affect your performance and the process by which you learn your skill.

Personality

Each person is unique and will respond differently in the same situation. This needs to be constantly considered when dealing with a performer.

Confidence

Belief in yourself is something that can change from day to day or from one situation to another. Confidence is essential for a good performance.

Motivation

Your motivation is your will to achieve success. A highly motivated person wants to achieve something and is prepared to sacrifice other things in order to achieve it. A person with low motivation is not really concerned whether they achieve something. Your motivation level is not the same for all activities, however, or even for all events within a certain activity. For example, some performers are not very motivated to train but are highly motivated during a competition. The level of motivation will also affect your skill learning process. For example, in a match a highly motivated person may decide to go for an interception or tackle. A less motivated person may not make the effort.

Factors affecting motivation include things that relate to the individual, such as their needs, expectations and their personality. There are also external factors that affect motivation such as the coach, possible rewards and the results or outcome of the performance.

Motivation may be:

- **intrinsic motivation** – someone does something for its own sake. The rewards to the person, such as enjoyment, self-satisfaction and feelings of achievement, are internal.

- **extrinsic motivation** – someone does something for external rewards. **Tangible rewards** are real, touchable things such as money, trophies or certificates. **Intangible rewards** cannot be felt or touched but are still rewarding, for example fame, social status and praise.

Performers can be motivated intrinsically, extrinsically or both. This depends a lot on their personality and the situation they are in. A lot of coaching schemes use badges and certificates to help motivate young people. However, those performers who are intrinsically motivated are more likely to stick at it. Although some of the top sports players earn a lot of money from their sport, many would say that they do it for the love of the sport and not for the money.

If you are motivated to succeed then you will be more concerned with performing well. Before an important performance, you may feel your heart beating faster, have sweaty palms and tense muscles. This is called **arousal** and can help you to perform well. However, if you become too aroused, or are not aroused enough, you may start to worry. This anxiety may make you feel threatened or you might see yourself failing. These feelings will have a negative effect on performance.

Sport psychologists

Many top performers now have sport psychologists working with them to help them with their psychological approach to training and performance.

Sport psychologists are specially trained to help performers learn various techniques that will improve their mental preparation. Sports psychologists will help performers to concentrate better, to relax and to be confident about themselves.

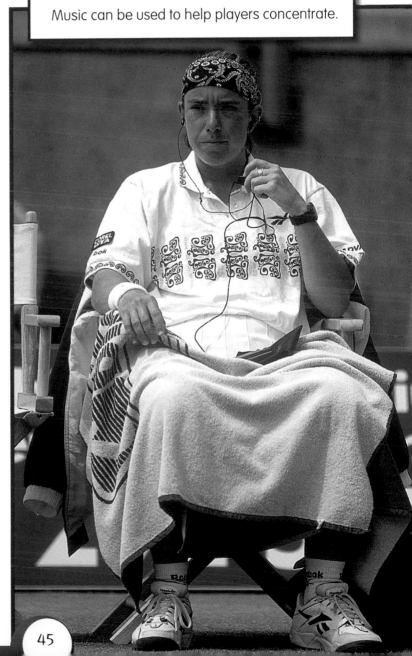

Music can be used to help players concentrate.

Glossary

aerobic endurance ability to keep exercising while using oxygen to supply energy

agility ability to perform rapidly a movement of the body, or part of it

amino acids simple units that make up protein, used for the manufacture of the structure of many tissues, haemoglobin, hormones and enzymes

anaerobic endurance ability to keep exercising without using oxygen

arousal feeling prior to an important performance that may make your heart beat faster and cause sweaty palms and tense muscles. It can help you to perform well.

balance ability to keep control of the body

body composition percentage of fat or lean body mass (anything that is not fat) that makes up the body

body fat total amount of fat in the body, usually expressed as a percentage

cardiovascular system heart and blood vessels, which transport blood around the body

complex carbohydrates (starches) carbohydrates made up of many sugar units (e.g. bread, rice, pasta and vegetables)

concentric contraction type of muscle contraction during which the muscle shortens as force is developed

coordination ability to put together a series of movements in an organized fashion, such as in a dance

dehydration when your body does not have enough water to work properly

duration length of time for a training session or work period

dynamic balance ability to maintain balance whilst moving (e.g. whilst ice skating)

dynamometer device to measure the force exerted against an immovable resistance

eccentric contraction type of muscle contraction during which the muscle lengthens as force is developed

ectomorph someone who has a thin and fragile body frame

endomorph someone who has a lot of fat that gives the body a rounded shape

essential amino acids amino acids that cannot be made by the body so must be obtained from the diet

extrinsic motivation when someone does something for external rewards

fast-twitch fibre type of muscle fibre that can produce more force than slow-twitch fibre but tires more rapidly

fat-soluble vitamins vitamins A, D, E and K that are stored in large quantities in your body

feedback information you receive about the result of an action that will affect how you do the action next time

fibre non-digestible carbohydrate that helps the digestive system function correctly

flexibility range of movement at a joint or series of joints

frequency number of training sessions per week

health-related fitness being fit in order to live a full and healthy life

information processing model model to explain what happens when learning or performing a skill

intangible rewards rewards that cannot be felt or touched, such as fame, social status and praise

intensity how hard the exercise is

intrinsic motivation when someone does something for its own sake, and the rewards, such as enjoyment, self-satisfaction and feelings of achievement, are internal

isometric contraction type of muscle contraction during which no movement occurs around a joint but force is still developed in the muscle

lean body mass (LBM) portion of body mass left when body fat has been subtracted from total body mass. It is made up of bones, muscles, blood and organs.

maximum oxygen uptake (VO_2 max) maximum amount of oxygen that the body can take in and use at any time

maximum strength maximum force produced in one effort

mesomorph someone who has a lot of muscle and a broad body frame

mode type of activity to be done (e.g. cycling)

monounsaturated fat type of fat found in peanut and olive oil

muscular endurance ability to perform repeated muscle contractions without tiring

nerve impulse electrical signal that sends information along a nerve

non-essential amino acids amino acids that can be made by the body

overload making a person or muscle work harder than normal in order to improve

overtraining when you train so hard that your body is unable to meet the demands of training

oxygen uptake (VO_2) amount of oxygen that your body takes in and uses at any time

perception process of interpreting and making sense of information received

performance-related fitness being fit in order to be able to do an activity as well as you can

polyunsaturated fat type of fat found in sunflower oil, soya bean oil and corn oil as well as in oily fish such as sardines

power combination of strength and speed. Power enables us to exert high levels of force over a short period of time.

progression as fitness improves, training needs to get harder to ensure overload is maintained and the performer continues to benefit

proprioception your ability to sense the position of parts of your body in space

psychology study of the mind and behaviour

repetition (rep) action of lifting and lowering a weight once, performed many times in succession, with no rest in between

reversibility when training is not maintained, and the benefits are lost

saturated fatty acid type of fat mainly found in animal products such as meat, poultry and dairy products

set number of repetitions, with rest periods in between

simple carbohydrates (sugars) carbohydrates consisting of a few sugar units (e.g. jam, marmalade, honey, sugar, sweets and biscuits)

skill ability to perform a movement correctly and efficiently most of the time

slow-twitch fibre type of muscle fibre that does not produce a lot of force but tires very slowly

somatotyping categorizing body type according to shape or form, without reference to size

specificity when the benefits of training are specific to the muscle group exercised or type of work performed

speed ability to move the body, or parts of it, quickly

speed endurance ability to perform repeated efforts without fatigue

sport scientist scientist who can give players and coaches advice on how to prepare mentally and/or physically for competition

static balance ability to hold the body in a stationary position

stimuli sources of information about things that are happening around us and inside us

stretching technique used to improve flexibility

stretch reflex reflex contraction of the muscle that occurs when a muscle is stretched quickly

tangible rewards rewards that are real, touchable things such as money, trophies or certificates

tapering process of gradually reducing training before an event so that carbohydrate stores are high

timing gates gates set up in pairs at the start and finish of a sprint to measure the time taken for the sprint

water-soluble vitamins vitamins B and C, mostly involved in energy production

Find out more

Books

Making Healthy Food Choices: Food for Sports, Neil Morris (Heinemann Library, 2006)

Making of a Champion: A World-Class Sprinter, Clive Gifford (Heinemann Library, 2005)

Websites

British Olympic Association: www.olympics.org.uk

Football Association: www.thefa.com

National Coaching Foundation: www.ncf.org.uk

Sport England: www.sportengland.org

Sports Coach: www.sportscoachuk.org

UK sport: www.uksport.gov.uk

World Anti Doping Agency: www.wada-ama.org

Index